WRITE RIGHT!

Writing POEMS

By Benjamin Proudfit

Gareth Stevens PUBLISHING

Please visit our website, www.garethstevens.com. For a free color catalog of all our high-quality books, call toll free 1-800-542-2595 or fax 1-877-542-2596.

Library of Congress Cataloging-in-Publication Data

Proudfit, Benjamin.
Writing poems / by Benjamin Proudfit.
p. cm. — (Write right!)
Includes index.
ISBN 978-1-4824-1125-6 (pbk.)
ISBN 978-1-4824-1126-3 (6-pack)
ISBN 978-1-4824-1124-9 (library binding)
1. Poetry — Authorship — Juvenile literature. 2. Creative writing — Juvenile literature. I. Title.
PN1042.P76 2015
808.1—d23

First Edition

Published in 2015 by
Gareth Stevens Publishing
111 East 14th Street, Suite 349
New York, NY 10003

Designer: Sarah Liddell
Editor: Kristen Rajczak

Photo credits: Cover, p. 1 © iStockphoto.com/aabejon; p. 5 Syda Productions/Shutterstock.com; p. 7 © iStockphoto.com/lisafx; p. 9 wavebreakmedia/Shutterstock.com; p. 11 Anna Jurkovska/Shutterstock.com; p. 13 justasc/Shutterstock.com; p. 15 (paper) CrackerClips/iStock/Thinkstock.com; p. 15 (background) stevanovicigor/iStock/Thinkstock.com; p. 17 Jacek Chabraszewski/Shutterstock.com; p. 19 © iStockphoto.com/Maica; p. 21 (background) mexrix/Shutterstock.com; p. 21 (boy) sashahaltam/Shutterstock.com.

Printed in the United States of America

CPSIA compliance information: Batch #CS15GS: For further information contact Gareth Stevens, New York, New York at 1-800-542-2595.

CONTENTS

Words in the glossary appear in **bold** type the first time they are used in the text.

WHAT IS A POEM?

For many school papers, you'll be asked to write using facts you've learned in class. You might even have to **research** a topic before you start to write.

But that's not the only kind of writing out there! In creative writing, such as in short stories, you get to use your imagination. Poetry is a kind of creative writing that commonly has rhyme, rhythm, and imagery. Keep reading to learn all about these features of a poem and how to write your own!

ON THE WRITE TRACK

What's your favorite song? Read the **lyrics** out loud—that's a poem!

Don't worry if you've never written a poem before. Creative writing is something everyone can do with a little work and imagination.

READ AND LEARN

Reading poetry others have written is a good way to learn about writing poems. The library has lots of poetry **anthologies** you can check out. You can look on the Internet for poetry to read, too.

Once you find a few poets you like, read books about their life. Writers are commonly **inspired** by things that happen to them. By learning about where a writer lived and worked, and what they liked to do, you might be able to find more meaning in their poems.

On the Write Track

Poems can be silly or serious. Read both kinds to find out which you might like to write.

If you're unsure about what poetry to read, ask your teacher, friends, parents, and older students what poets they like!

MATCHING SOUNDS

"Fine" sounds like "dine." "Letter" sounds like "better." These words have the same sound—they rhyme! Many poems use rhyming words.

Sometimes, poems use a pattern of rhyming words. In the example below, the first and second lines rhyme and the third and fourth lines rhyme.

Humpty Dumpty sat on a wall.
Humpty Dumpty had a great fall.
All the king's horses and all the king's men
Couldn't put Humpty together again.

On the Write Track

One of the coolest things about poetry is that you can make up spellings of words or choose not to use **punctuation**. Still, it's a good idea to write in complete sentences first to make sure your meaning is clear.

One row of words in a poem is called a line. It might be a complete sentence, but it can also be part of a sentence that continues onto the next line. It may be just one word, too.

GIVE IT SOME RHYTHM

Just like in music, poems often have rhythm. Rhythm is the ordered pattern of accented and unaccented **syllables**. An accent is the part of the word that's said with more **emphasis**. Say the word "party" out loud. The first part of the word is accented: PAR-ty. Try to put the accent on the second syllable. It sounds funny!

The nursery rhyme used on page 8, "Humpty Dumpty," has rhythm. Say it slowly aloud. Can you hear which parts of words you're emphasizing?

On the Write Track

A line break is the place a writer chooses to end a line in a poem. Line breaks can be used to surprise the reader or add importance to a word or idea.

When making music or dancing, the rhythm sets how the song or dance feels—fast, slow, or somewhere between the two. You can use as much or as little rhythm in a poem as you'd like.

FOLLOW THE FORM

Some poems follow a form, or the set of rules used for writing a kind of poem. The rules might be about which words have to rhyme, how many lines the poem will be, or the rhythm of the poem.

One kind of form poem is a haiku (HY-koo). It has three lines. The first and third lines have five syllables. The second line has seven. This is a nonrhyming poem form.

A cooler wind blows.
Wings move through the fading light.
The summer birds leave.

ON THE WRITE TRACK

The last line of a haiku is often an observation about what you're writing about.

Haikus are usually about nature.

WHAT'S IT ABOUT?

Very often, writers use poetry to **express** their feelings. Sadness, anger, and disappointment are common topics. So are happiness and excitement.

But you can write a poem about anything! A poem can tell a story or **describe** something. Writers sometimes use a poem to say how two things are the same or different. One poem by William Shakespeare begins, "Shall I compare thee to a summer's day?" In addition, your poem can be about something real or something imaginary!

ON THE WRITE TRACK

Write a poem pretending to be a cat, a train, or a tree. You'll really have to use your imagination to tell what it's like being something other than yourself!

This is an acrostic (uh-KRAWS-tihk) poem. It uses the letters in a word or name as the beginning of words that describe the word or name.

Sassy
Always happy
Musical
Athletic
Not shy
Talkative
Honest
Approachable

START WRITING

Once you've decided what you want to write about, doing some brainstorming or freewriting can be helpful. Both of these can also help you pick a topic if you haven't thought of one yet!

Freewriting is just what it sounds like—writing freely. Sit down in a quiet place and just write, either about your chosen topic or whatever comes to mind. After a few minutes, read over what you've written. Are there any lines or ideas you like?

ON THE WRITE TRACK

One way to brainstorm for poem writing is to make a list of words that rhyme. You could also make a list of words that make you think of a topic, such as summer, a friend, or your dog.

If you're having trouble writing, take a walk. Look at the world around you. Or you can close your eyes and daydream a little!

CHOOSE WISELY

When you're writing description in your poem, paint a picture with your words. Is the air cold or frigid? What color is the cloud—white or ivory? All your descriptions are called imagery. Using interesting, **specific** imagery makes your "word painting" grow before the reader's eyes!

Take time to choose the right verbs, or action words, in your poem, too. Here's a list of common verbs and some **synonyms** you could use instead:

run	sprint, jog, trot
eat	gobble, feast, inhale
scream	screech, roar, wail

ON THE WRITE TRACK

A thesaurus is a useful tool for a poet! It has entries like a dictionary, but instead of a definition, this book lists a word's synonyms.

Word choice is an important part of writing your poem. Unusual descriptive words, or adjectives, can surprise and delight your reader and make your meaning clearer.

TIME TO REVISE

A poem can have just three lines, like a haiku, or be many pages long! When you've written all you want to, it's time to go back and revise, or make changes. This may include fixing any rhyme or rhythm pattern problems, adding imagery, and checking spelling and punctuation.

Revising poetry that's about your feelings can be hard. Sometimes it's a good idea to set a poem aside for awhile before you look at it to revise. You'll have a fresh point of view when you read it again!

ON THE WRITE TRACK

If you're especially proud of a poem, share it! Read it out loud to your class, give it to your mom, or have a poetry reading where your friends all share poems, too.

WHAT SHOULD I WRITE ABOUT?

a day in the life of a dog

your first home run

a story your grandpa told you

a thunderstorm

the last day of summer vacation

what it's like to taste mom's apple pie

GLOSSARY

anthology: a collection of writing, such as short stories or poems

describe: to write about

emphasis: a special force given to a syllable

express: to make known

inspire: to cause someone to want to do something

lyrics: the words of a song

punctuation: the marks, such as periods (.) and commas (,), that are used to make the meaning of a piece of writing clear

research: studying to find something new

specific: exact or detailed

syllable: an individual sound that combines with other sounds to make up a word in spoken language

synonym: a word having the same or almost the same meaning

FOR MORE INFORMATION

BOOKS

Ganeri, Anita. *Poems*. Chicago, IL: Heinemann Library, 2013.

Kalz, Jill. *Tickles, Pickles, and Floofing Persnickles: Reading and Writing Nonsense Poems*. North Mankato, MN: Picture Window Books, 2014.

WEBSITES

The Children's Poetry Archive
poetryarchive.org/childrensarchive/home.do
Read or listen to many different poems, and read about the poets who wrote them.

Giggle Poetry
gigglepoetry.com
Read poems, play games, and learn more about poetry on this website.

Publisher's note to educators and parents: Our editors have carefully reviewed these websites to ensure that they are suitable for students. Many websites change frequently, however, and we cannot guarantee that a site's future contents will continue to meet our high standards of quality and educational value. Be advised that students should be closely supervised whenever they access the Internet.

INDEX